44

Ways to Strengthen Your Marriage

44

Ways to Strengthen Your Marriage

Jerry Drace
Foreword by Henry Blackaby

DOVE INSPIRATIONAL PRESS
GRETNA 2007

Library of Congress Cataloging-in-Publication Data

Drace, Jerry.
 44 ways to strengthen your marriage / Jerry Drace ; foreword by Henry Blackaby.
  p. cm.
 ISBN-13: 978-1-58980-505-7 (pbk. : alk. paper) 1. Spouses—Prayers and devotions. 2. Marriage—Religious aspects—Christianity. I. Title: Forty-four ways to strengthen your marriage. II. Title.
 BV4596.M3D68 2007
 248.8'44—dc22
                                2007016160

Printed in the United States of America

Published by Dove Inspirational Press, an imprint of
  Pelican Publishing Company, Inc.
1000 Burmaster Street, Gretna, Louisiana 70053

Contents

Foreword

Marriage is under severe attack in the nation today! All forms of media are disparaging marriage, and especially the Christian expression of God's intended eternal purpose and place of marriage in society.

Christian marriages are also being drastically affected, with divorce rising at an alarming rate. This book comes at a most strategic moment, and can, if followed, do much to strengthen today's marriages and homes. We need specific guidance, and this is carefully offered here.

I highly recommend this timely book to all, and especially to marriage counselors, pastors, and all who are seeking to strengthen marriage.

HENRY BLACKABY

Preface

In 1993, I wrote pastors throughout the United States and asked them one question, "What is the greatest need in your church?" When all the replies were examined, the number one response by far was, "How do I minister to the needs of the families in my church?" Out of this simple question was born Hope for the Home, a vital part of the ministry of the Jerry Drace Evangelistic Association.

As one pastor said after a Hope for the Home conference in his church, "This has been one of the greatest events in the life of this church. Hope for the Home goes right to the heart of the challenges facing our families regardless of their age, race, education, or economic positions. I know it has made a tremendous impact on my life as a husband and father."

Introduction

No one is an expert on marriage except the one who has never been married. The same applies to experts on potty training, raising children, teenage dating, and every other aspect of family life. There are no experts in the arena of marriage, only practitioners. The following suggestions on how to strengthen your marriage come from the Hope for the Home conferences that my wife and I have conducted throughout the United States and Great Britain since 1993.

Thousands of husbands and wives have contributed to this marriage primer. It is a primer simply because it is short and to the point. However, each of the forty-four recommendations will take your marriage farther and keep it united longer than the 50 percent of new marriages that end in divorce. Marriage requires more than paper plates and Styrofoam convenience. It demands fine china and crystal commitment.

I suggest you read *44 Ways to Strengthen Your Marriage* separately and then together with your spouse. You will notice at the end of each chapter there are two Bible verses. One is from the Old Testament and the other from the New Testament. The purpose is for both of you to read these together. Husbands, let me strongly suggest that you read the one from the Old Testament. It is a wise husband who does not ask his wife to do anything with the word "old" in it.

After you have read the verses there is a section for you to reflect in your own words what the verses mean to you. Then I have included an interaction section for you to take what you have just read and relate it to your marriage.

May God bless you and give you insight in your desire to strengthen your marriage. This book will be worth handing down to your children. In fact, I suggest that you get extra copies to give each child on their wedding day. It will be here sooner than you think. I know from experience. Remember, "unless the LORD builds the house, they labor in vain who build it" (Ps. 127:1).

1

Care for Your Spouse

If I were to ask you, "What is the opposite of love?" you would probably say, "Hate." Most people think of love and hate as being extreme opposites. However, in listening to couples whose marriages are coming apart at the seams I am convinced the opposite of love is indifference. Love is a feeling, and so is hate. Both are intense. Indifference, however, is a suspended state of all feelings. It neither loves nor hates. It says to the other spouse, "I could care less if you fell off the face of the earth," as one hurting husband put it.

Indifference. Apathy. Lukewarm. These are words that describe the opposite of love. Or, Laodicean, as described in the Bible in Revelation 3:16. Any way you look at it, these tepid responses to a spouse are an unspoken statement that the marriage is in deep trouble. The antidote for this poison is care.

When you care for your spouse, you are concerned about every area of their life for "as long as you both shall live." The excitement of the heart-pounding love of the dating days and the intensity of emotions of the engagement days will not be sufficient to carry you through the weathered years of marriage. Care transcends feelings, which are based on emotions, and stands firm in the face of any and all forces that would seek to undermine marriage. Care says, "I will never intentionally hurt you or neglect you. I will not allow indifference to creep into our relationship." This commitment requires constant vigilance. As you would guard and care for a valuable work of art, so much more should you care for the priceless journey of marriage.

One dear couple I heard about from North Providence, Rhode Island, has been married eighty-two years. When asked what had kept them together so long, the husband replied, "Patience and understanding." In other words, they cared for each other.

Read

Song of Solomon 8:6-7, "Love is as strong as death, jealousy as cruel as the grave. . . . Many waters cannot quench love, nor can the floods drown it."

Ephesians 5:29, "For no one ever hated his own flesh, but nourishes and cherishes it, just as the Lord does the church."

Reflect

Handwritten notes:

Heinrich | Robbie

- listening (spontaneous)
- Being affectionate
- overlooking things
- ~~(crossed out)~~

- Doing things I enjoy
- Try to do the things that bother (rinse dishes)
- Compliment

Relate

Ask your spouse how you can better care for them. What can each of you do to show more expressions of caring for each other? Share different ways you can guard your marriage from falling into the trap of mediocrity and indifference.

2

Consider Your Spouse over Others

How often have you been in a situation where you observed a spouse being neglected? It may have been at a social affair, church service, or sporting event; nevertheless, the pain of being slighted was registered on their face. Very few things in life make an individual feel more unloved and unwanted than being overlooked by the person they are with, especially if it is their spouse. Make sure your spouse is included in every introduction. Make them feel they are a vital part of your everyday experiences.

Do you remember your dating days? They were filled with expectancy, excitement, and electricity. You could hardly wait to be in the presence of the one you loved. Why then has this once heart-throbbing, pulse-pounding relationship become stagnant, stale, and sedate? One reason is that you started excluding each other in your most important decisions and outside activities. The one you always wanted to be with should always be the one you want to be with. Do not allow a friend or group of friends to gradually take you away from the one who took you away from the others in the first place. Your spouse may give verbal approval for your absence and neglect, while silently screaming, "Pay some attention to me!" You can be in the same room with your husband or wife and not be with them. As one wife stated, "My husband wants me with him at all his social functions and gatherings because I am attractive and a good listener. However, he never includes me personally in his conversation with others. I might just as well be in another room." Your personal consideration is required. Otherwise, someone else will be glad to give your spouse the attention they are craving.

Read

Proverbs 5:15, "Drink water from your own cistern, and running water from your own well."

John 15:12, "This is My commandment, that you love one another as I have loved you."

Reflect

Robbie	Hannah
When Hannah sit is in the backseat w/ Abby /putting the baby before Robbie	At home in the living room /separet. at night during bed - seperate no romance

Relate

How can you make your spouse feel special when you two are in a social setting? Ask your spouse to share the last time they felt neglected or left out (do not defend yourself). Talk about the activities that brought you together in the first place. Plan one of those events again, just the two of you. Agree to give priority to each other when in the company of others.

3

Trust Each Other

What is the opposite of trust? Simple, it is distrust. When spouses do not trust each other, the relationship reverts back to high school dating. Remember how you would always ask the object of your infatuation who they sat by at lunch, who did they talk to after class, who they saw at the mall? All the "who" questions are like a flock of geese always pecking at the heels. After awhile it gets annoying. If you do not trust your husband or wife, you can not have a solid marriage. It is like trying to live in a brick house without any mortar between the bricks. It will stand only until a door is slammed or a strong wind blows up.

Just as trust in Jesus brings God greater glory than anything else you can provide, so does trust in your spouse. Trust is earned. It can be neither demanded nor dictated. As intentionally as it takes to build the bonds of trust, those bonds can instantly be broken by a selfish act. Even when someone breaks our trust it should not drive us into the barren fields where the weeds of doubt, skepticism, and suspicion take root in our souls.

C. S. Lewis stated, "To love involves trusting the beloved beyond the evidence, even against much evidence." Trust walks hand in hand with faith. When the vows are exchanged, the foundation of trust is laid on which the house of marriage will be built. The only way to make sure that house will remain standing is to never crack the foundation.

Read

Proverbs 31:11, "The heart of her husband safely trusts her; so he will have no lack of gain."

1 Peter 4:8, "And above all things have fervent love for one another, for 'love will cover a multitude of sins.'"

Reflect

N/A

Relate

Discuss with your spouse the meaning of the word "trust." Have you ever given your spouse reason to mistrust you? If so, have you taken the necessary steps to restore that trust? Share the similarities between trust and faith. Reread the statement by C. S. Lewis and talk about its meaning in your marriage.

4

Promote Each Other's Spiritual Growth

When most couples return from their honeymoon their thoughts are seldom on spiritual matters. They have to furnish the apartment or home, if they are blessed to have one at such an early stage of their marriage. They may be involved in finishing their education. Finding a job may be the first order of business. Securing insurance and health care for each other is important. Before they know it, all the new requirements have crowded out the most essential, which is the spiritual growth of the marriage.

The Bible is still the greatest handbook on the "how tos" of marriage. It will get you through the first year and carry you through "as long as you both shall live." You should begin each day together with a verse of scripture and a prayer. It is more important than breakfast because it will feed you throughout the day. You should end each day with a verse of scripture and a prayer. It is more important than sex because it will satisfy you throughout the night.

A balanced marriage is like an equilateral triangle. One side is the sexual. One side is the sensual or emotional. The foundational side is the spiritual. It is an amazing fact in marriage that if both the husband and wife are growing together spiritually, they will experience the same results sexually and sensually. However, if the spiritual side is neglected, the other two sides become unequal and therefore out of balance.

A couple I once counseled had not been sexually intimate for several years yet was in church every Sunday. The husband shared that his wife had no desire for the sexual side of the triangle model and that the sensual side was practically nonexistent as well. In this case the spiritual foundation was one-sided and as a result the marriage was under a great deal of strain to say the least.

God intended the husband and wife to experience all that is good and morally pleasurable. This can only be fully realized in your marriage when you promote each other's spiritual growth. Many have the lop-sided view that the more spiritual they become the less interest they will have in sex. God told Adam and Eve, "Be fruitful and multiply" (Gen. 1:28). He did not say, "Be spiritual and subtract." To deny the necessity of any side of the triangle is to create a polygon, which is unbalanced.

Read

1 Samuel 1:19, "Then they rose early in the morning and worshiped before the LORD."

Romans 14:19, "Therefore let us pursue the things which make for peace and the things by which one may edify another."

Reflect

[handwritten: matt.]

_[handwritten: Read Bible 10 min. J of Scrip-time in morning alone and devo ____ night together.]_

Relate

Discuss the triangle model of marriage with your spouse. Is there balance in each of the three sides? What can you do to improve the foundational side, which is the spiritual? Talk about the things that you are pursuing in your marriage and rate them in order of priority.

[handwritten: 1 - spiritual life
2 - hobby
3 - home / finances]

5

Worship as a Family

Church can be one of the loneliest places on earth for a spouse if the other spouse is out "doing their thing." It is puzzling to the children when Daddy pulls up in front of the church, lets everyone out, and then drives off. It speaks volumes to them, especially the boys. Also, equally disturbing is when the husband goes to one church and the wife attends another. Not only does it rob them of much needed time together, it also steals the experience of communal worship. They may be worshiping individually, but God intends for the family to experience Him collectively as well.

Husbands and wives who worship together have a common bond in their spiritual growth. If there are children in the family, then an even deeper dimension is added to the worship experience. A husband once confided in me that for years he took their son to his church while his wife took their daughter to her church. As the children were entering high school he realized through a series of events that the family was split over some very important moral issues due to the teachings of his church. This father admittedly confessed to his lack of spiritual leadership in the home and finally realized that his church was very slack in both the preaching and teaching of sound biblical principles. Uniting together as a family and attending a church where the Word of God was preached and taught without compromise brought his children through their crisis.

You have heard it said, "A family that prays together stays together." This is most likely true. Also, it is equally true that a family that worships together grows together. With such a variety of worship styles available, choosing one that will meet the desires of each family member maybe a challenge. Just remember that it is not about you, your spouse, or your children. It is all about encountering the presence of God. Do not allow the style of worship to dictate your place of worship. When you are more concerned about the expression rather than the experience, you have already missed the purpose.

Worshiping as a family in a Bible-centered, Christ-honoring, Spirit-led church where the staff are men and women of integrity is more important than programs and personalities. Equally important is that what you experience in church on Sunday you exhibit at home Monday through Saturday.

Read

Psalm 107:32, "Let them exalt Him also in the congregation of the people, and praise Him in the assembly of the elders."

Hebrews 10:25, "Not forsaking the assembling of ourselves together, as is the manner of some, but exhorting one another, and so much the more as you see the Day approaching."

Reflect

Strengths	weaknesses

Relate

Talk with your spouse about their feelings regarding the church where you worship. What are its strengths and its weaknesses? If you are attending separate churches, discuss the possibility of worshiping together and what it would take to bring that possibility to reality.

6

Let Submission Begin with the Husband

Most husbands will tell you they are the heads of their homes whether it is true or not. As one husband said, "If you don't believe that I am the head of my house, ask my wife. She told me I was."

The Bible gives great insight into the man named Noah. It tells us he was, "a just man, perfect in his generations," and that he "walked with God" (Gen. 6:9). This means he was upright and honest. He was a man of moral integrity. He was a husband and father who consistently pleased God. In other words, Noah earned the right to be the head of his family and captain of the ark.

If a husband must shout at his wife to get his point across and bark at his children to obtain their obedience, then basically he is just a loud husband who acts like a dog. Being at the front of the pack doesn't necessarily qualify as being the lead dog. Leadership is earned; especially spiritual leadership.

"Submission" is one of the most misunderstood words in all of Holy Scripture. It has been used to bring "the little wife" into subjection and "the little urchins" into servitude. Submission as found in Ephesians 5:22 means voluntary submission based on a commitment to proper order. The order of human creation finds God creating man first and then woman second. This placed the woman, Eve, in a subordinate but not subservient position to her husband, Adam. Man was created to be guided from his head, and woman was created to be guided from her heart. Satan tempted Eve through her heart by deception, and Eve tempted Adam through his head by disobedience. The result was expulsion from paradise.

If the husband submits to Christ and loves his wife as Christ loves the church (Eph. 5:25), then there will most likely be harmony in the home. What wife would not want to be treated in the same manner that Christ treats his bride?

Submission is voluntary. It is based on a commitment to proper order, much like skydiving. The proper order is that you jump, then voluntarily pull the rip cord. It's your choice. No one can make you, but if you refuse to open the parachute, the results will be disastrous.

Read

Genesis 6:9, "This is the genealogy of Noah. Noah was a just man, perfect in his generations. Noah walked with God."

Ephesians 5:22 and 33, "Wives, submit to your own husbands, as to the Lord. Nevertheless let each one of you in particular so love his own wife as himself, and let the wife see that she respects her husband."

Reflect

_____

_____

_____

_____

Relate

Discuss with your spouse the meaning of submission in today's culture. Talk about it in light of the scriptures above and in relation to my definition based on Ephesians 5:22. How are submission and servanthood related? Is there any area in your marriage where submission is a real challenge? If so, share it with your spouse in a caring, loving way.

7

Encourage Your Spouse to Spread Their Wings

A bird born in the wild that never flies is never seen or heard. The same applies to an individual who never leaves the nest of complacency for the world of wonder. The "wish I hads" will be of little comfort when the days turn into weeks and the weeks into years and you look into the rearview mirror of life only to have regrets for the things you did not attempt. If you float down the river of life in the same current as your dreams, you will always be in view of those dreams, but will never be able to capture them. Put your oar into the water and paddle. Encourage your spouse to become all God created them to be by helping them row.

When God created man and woman, he made them in his image (Gen. 1:27). This means that a husband and wife have moral and spiritual abilities that need to be developed to maturity. Your spouse has emotions, intellect, and will that need to be expressed. Your marriage will have greater and deeper dimensions when you both seek to inspire each other's gifts and talents.

A wife shared with my wife how her husband was her best cheerleader and how much his encouragement contributed to strengthening their marriage. Never be fearful or threatened by the accomplishments of your spouse as long as they maintain their priorities. You are a team. Victory is sweeter when celebrated together.

Read

Genesis 1:27, "So God created man in His own image; in the image of God He created him; male and female He created them."

1 Thessalonians 5:11, "Therefore comfort each other and edify one another, just as you also are doing."

Reflect

_____

_____

_____

_____

Relate

Is there something you have always wanted to accomplish and have yet to attempt it? Share it with your spouse. Do not be fearful of their response. This is your dream. How can you help your spouse fulfill their dream? Discuss some of the "what ifs" and dismiss the "wish I hads."

8

Compliment Your Spouse in Public

A word of praise and appreciation for your spouse in front of others not only affirms them, it also speaks volumes about the strength of your marriage. There is nothing more uplifting and inspiring than to hear your name spoken by your spouse in complimentary terms. Remember your dating days. You could not say enough sweet things about the object of your love. The same should be true after marriage.

Words, while small, carry such great weight. They can raise your mate's self-image to its highest power, like the little numerators over the larger denominators. Your words like "little drops of water, little grains of sand, make the mighty ocean and the pleasant land" (Julia Fletcher, "Little Things," 1845). Never underestimate the power and impact of the spoken word.

Solomon knew the importance of a well-chosen word when he said, "A word fitly spoken is like apples of gold in settings of silver" (Prov. 25:11). Words of praise will take your marriage farther and keep it sweeter longer than all the gifts you can purchase.

Husbands, it is not the classical words that wives love to hear. It is the romantic words like "diamonds," "emeralds," "pearls," "rubies," and "sapphires." If you can't afford to purchase these little sparkling words, do what I do, show your wife a picture of these jewels and tell her that if you could, you would buy her one of each, but even then they would not excel her beauty. It could make for a great night.

Read

Proverbs 31:10, 30, 31, "Who can find a virtuous wife? For her worth is far above rubies. . . . Charm is deceitful and beauty is vain, but a woman who fears the LORD, she shall be praised. Give her of the fruit of her hands, and let her own works praise her in the gates."

Philippians 1:3, "I thank my God upon every remembrance of you."

Reflect

[handwritten notes:]
hardworking | good mom
strong | hard working @ school
smart | organized schedule + dates + time
kind | honest
beard | communicate

Relate

Tonight instead of watching television try this as a couple. Make a list of ten words that you feel describe your best qualities. Then swap lists with each other. Memorize each other's top ten and begin to use those words of praise at home and in public. It will strengthen your friendship and your marriage.

9

Be Willing to Apologize

I once had a secretary who said her father never apologized to anyone even when he knew he was wrong. He once went six weeks without speaking to her mother until she apologized for what was clearly his fault. When an individual will never apologize and admit they are sorry for their actions, there is one word to describe that person, "Sorry." That type of spouse will eventually become alienated from everyone who ever loved them and in all likelihood will end up living alone in the winter years of life.

Children who grow up in a home where one or both parents are discourteous, disrespectful, impolite, and insensitive may exhibit these same characteristics in their marriages. The cycle can be broken by replacing these ill-mannered traits with those that promote unity rather than division.

The mature spouse will accept responsibility for the hurt and the healing of the relationship. The road of marriage will not always be well paved and straight. There will be curves, detours, footpaths, mountain passes, trails, and tunnels that must be negotiated. It is so easy in our society to just forsake one journey for another, one spouse for another. The destination is well worth the effort, and the directions found in God's Word will never lead anyone astray. A sincere apology will lead to redemption, which will bring about restoration. Better is a marriage restored than one destroyed.

Read

Isaiah 5:21, "Woe to those who are wise in their own eyes, and prudent in their own sight!"

James 4:10, "Humble yourselves in the sight of the Lord, and He will lift you up."

Reflect

_____

_____

_____

_____

Relate

Is there anything for which you need to apologize to your spouse or perhaps your children? Are you using situations in the past to excuse your unwillingness to apologize in the present? Read the two Bible verses again and discuss the reflections you wrote down with your spouse. If healing needs to take place in your marriage, this is the place to start.

10

Be Willing to Forgive

How often has one spouse said to another, "I forgive you," only to bring up the past occurrence at some future date?

A husband related to me about his wife's infidelity, "I told her I forgave her. I buried the hatchet, but I did not bury the handle. Every time we got into an argument I pulled out the past." We do not fully forgive until the handle is buried. "I forgive you" is one of the most powerful expressions a human can extend toward another. It is often pride and self-centeredness that prevent the guilty party from accepting this priceless gift.

Forgiveness is a choice. In the context of marriage you can either forgive or retaliate. Seldom in marriage is it necessary to resort to the use of force. Even in the event of spousal abuse it is better to depart from the situation and allow the law enforcement officials to take charge. Forgiveness will make you better. The opposite will make you bitter.

A young wife shared with me that she found her husband and her best friend in bed together in their own home. For two years she plotted his murder in such a way that no one would find out who had committed the crime. One morning as she was looking in the mirror putting on her makeup she took an intense look at her face. She noticed that hate lines had developed around her eyes. Deep wrinkles had formed around her lips. She had aged almost ten years in just that short period of time. She said with tears flowing down her cheeks, "I realized I was so full of hate and bitterness that the only one I was killing was myself." At that point she began to study forgiveness throughout the Bible. After several weeks she asked God to remove the hurt, anger, and resentment in her life and fill her heart with peace and forgiveness. Immediately the load she had been carrying was lifted, and a sweet peace filled her heart. Going to the house where her husband and her friend were living together, she knocked on the door. When he opened it, she told him that she no longer hated him or her friend and that she forgave them for what they had done to her and their marriage. She then turned and walked away with peace in her heart because she had made the choice to forgive.

There are five excellent benefits of forgiveness: (1) Forgiveness breaks the cycle of blame and pain. You no longer are controlled by your past. (2) Forgiveness removes the anger and guilt. You no longer react out of resentment and shame. (3) Forgiveness places the offended on the same side as the offender. You realize that you are capable of hurting others and that some-day you may need to be forgiven. (4) Forgiveness is an act of faith. You leave the consequences up to God. (5) Forgiveness is a choice. You can either remain imprisoned by the past or be set free for your future. Understand that just because forgiveness is extended doesn't mean it will be received. That too is a choice.

Read

Psalm 86:5, "For You, Lord, are good, and ready to forgive, and abundant in mercy to all those who call upon You."

Romans 12:19, "Beloved, do not avenge yourselves, but rather give place to wrath; for it is written, 'Vengeance is Mine, I will repay,' says the Lord."

Reflect

_____

_____

_____

_____

Relate

Do you need to extend forgiveness to your spouse? If so, get alone together and share your willingness to extend this greatest of all Christian virtues. The true test of forgiveness is that once it is extended it is never rescinded. Do you need to forgive yourself? If God has forgiven you, then you can do the same.

11

Let Your Spouse
Have Some Personal Time

Everyone needs some personal time once in a while. For us husbands we often take our personal time on the golf course, in the workshop, in the duck blind, in the bass boat, or a hundred other places we go to unwind. Wives are no different. They also need time for recreation, relaxation, and renewal.

If your wife works outside the home, then she puts in as many hours a week at her job as do you on yours. If your wife is a stay-at-home spouse and mother, then she certainly needs some free time for herself each week. I am not talking about several hours away from you and the children, but periods where she can enjoy her hobby or favorite pastime.

In our home, if my wife, Becky, is in her sewing room (or "creative expression area" as I refer to it), then I know she is in her element and needs that time to be alone. When she is in our bathroom and the Jacuzzi is humming, I know she is unwinding from a hectic day and needs some time to herself. Once in a while she will meet one of her friends for lunch where they catch up on each other's lives and schedules.

Let me be quick to add, I feel strongly that you and your spouse need to have a hobby or sport you enjoy doing together. Some of our most memorable times have been skiing on the slopes watching our children a mile in front of us. We have enjoyed long walks on the beach searching for shark teeth while the children were chasing great whites. The personal times make the together times that much more special.

Read

Proverbs 3:27, "Do not withhold good from those to whom it is due, when it is in the power of your hand to do so."

1 Corinthians 16:14, "Let all that you do be done with love."

Reflect

_____

_____

_____

_____

Relate

Give your spouse a gift certificate to their favorite getaway place. It might be a round of golf at his favorite course, or it might be a morning at her favorite spa. After this special personal time, get together for a special dinner with just the two of you and share the day's experience. Doing this on a regular basis will create anticipation and expectation.

12

Remember: Communication Is the Name of the Game

The number one complaint among married couples is the breakdown in communication after the first few years. The latest survey shows that couples talk with each other about seventy minutes per day during their first year of marriage. Those minutes are reduced by 20 percent each succeeding year until the eighth year. It is amazing that during the dating days couples talk all the time. After the marriage, talking drops off, and silence picks up. What was once a chattering marathon becomes a speechless stalemate.

This doesn't have to happen. Those conversing times before the marriage must continue after the ceremony. Your commitment to time with each other is as important as your vows of faithfulness to each other.

Women thrive on conversation with their husbands because it says, "You really care about me and my feelings." Men feel that conversation is unnecessary because they show their love and concern by their actions.

Both men and women talk, but generally they are different in what they talk about. Men talk mostly about external things. Women talk mostly about internal things. Men talk cars. Women talk children. Men talk football. Women talk families. Men talk shop. Women talk shopping. It seems to some women that men grunt. It seems to some men that women gush. It is not that difficult to understand why they have problems communicating.

This is why it is so important to develop the habit of talking and listening to each other after the honeymoon. Great communication requires both elements. Husbands, we need to realize that for most of us our vocabulary is half that of our wives. This means we need to either listen twice as much or buy a dictionary and learn some new words.

One wife said, "My husband has turned into a Neanderthal. All he ever does when he gets home from work is get the paper, turn on the television, sit down in his favorite chair, and start grunting. He sounds like a caveman." Here was a wife who was living in the Information Age with a husband who was still enjoying the Stone Age.

Communication involves more than the verbal exchange of words. Body language is as important as what is spoken. Ralph Waldo Emerson once said, "When the eyes say one thing and the tongue another, a practiced man relies on the language of the first." This rule applies to a practiced husband and wife as well. Often we may be agreeing with our tongue, but our posture is saying the opposite. Those sign languages before marriage days still speak volumes after the marriage. It has been recently documented that spouses spend less than three minutes of meaningful conversation together in a typical day. It takes discipline to continue communicating after the vows are spoken, but it is well worth the effort. When the lines of communication are broken, the marriage vows are soon to follow.

Read

Psalm 37:30, "The mouth of the righteous speaks wisdom, and his tongue talks of justice."

Matthew 15:11, "Not what goes into the mouth defiles a man; but what comes out of the mouth, this defiles a man."

Reflect

_____

_____

_____

_____

Relate

Talk to your spouse about the things that initially attracted you to them. Ask them what qualities attracted them to you. Spend an evening sharing your best memories of the past and your hopes and dreams for the future. Be sure to listen with your eyes as well as your ears. Plan a time each week where you and your spouse do nothing but talk and listen to each other concerning your feelings about the challenges taking place in your marriage and family. Listen intently. Speak carefully.

13

Listen to Your Spouse

This is the hardest thing to do in the area of communication. Usually we are either preparing our reply when our spouse is talking, or tuning them out altogether. Listening requires intense concentration.

The older couple was walking through the woods one afternoon, and the man turned to his wife and said, "It's windy, isn't it?" She replied, "No it's Thursday." He paused a moment and said, "Me too, let's get something to drink."

Sometimes neither party listens. A vital part of listening is also looking. Researchers have found that complete communication is 7 percent words, 38 percent tone of voice, and 55 percent nonverbal. In other words, what our bodies say is more important than what our voices say. Look at your spouse when they are talking to you just as you did in your dating days. Listen with your ears and your eyes.

Sometimes silence is the best part of communication as illustrated by a story told to me by a friend who was a highway patrolman. He pulled over a man for speeding on the interstate. As he approached the car he noticed the radio was so loud the car was rocking. When the driver rolled down the window my friend said, "Do you know you were driving ninety miles per hour?" The driver's wife said, "He always drives fast." My patrolman friend noticed the driver was not wearing his seat belt. When he asked him about it the wife said, "He never wears his seat belt." Then my friend said, "How could you hear me with your radio so loud?" Again the wife said, "He always plays it loud." The driver turned to his wife and shouted, "Will you shut up!" My friend then looked across the car at her and said, "Ma'am, does he always talk to you like that?" She replied, "Nope, only when he's been drinking!" Sometimes it's just best not to say anything.

The art of listening is seldom mastered by most people. The reason is that we are basically lazy. We had rather ask the person to repeat themselves, or we act on what we thought we heard. This failure to listen affects every relationship from home to business and everything in between. Taking the time to listen will alleviate many conflicts in marriage as well as all the other relationships we encounter along the way.

Read

Proverbs 2:2, "Incline your ear to wisdom, and apply your heart to understanding."

Colossians 4:6, "Let your speech always be with grace, seasoned with salt, that you may know how you ought to answer each one."

Reflect

_____

_____

_____

_____

Relate

What can you and your spouse do to practice the art of listening? Take a walk this afternoon if possible and just listen to the sounds around you without speaking. When the walk is finished discuss the various sounds you heard. If you can attune your ears to hear the sounds around you, you can listen even more intently to each other.

14

Schedule Special Time to Be with Each Other

There can not be a meeting of the hearts if the hearts never meet.

A wife who has a professional career as well as a husband wrote to us and said, "As I mature I think more and more about the friendships that we seem to be content to let fade quietly away; and about the real joys we are missing in life. Materialism has subtly consumed so much of our lives that we hardly know what has happened. Our jobs monopolize our time—so much so that there seems little time, if any, for caring about people, or for building and maintaining relationships." I fear that someday we will receive a letter stating that their marriage has also faded quietly away.

The shortness of time and the length of eternity must not be forgotten. Like it or not, we must schedule special, uninterrupted time for our spouse. The babies will be fine for three or four hours with a babysitter or grandparents. The babysitter and grandparents may be sitting in a corner mumbling to themselves when you get back, but it's worth a try. Leave the cell phone at home and just do something special. A dear little lady who had been married for more than fifty years told my wife that she and her husband did three special things throughout all their years of marriage. They dialogued daily, dated weekly, and departed quarterly. If it worked for their marriage, it will probably work for yours and mine.

Read

Ecclesiastes 3:1, "To everything there is a season, a time for every purpose under heaven."

Ephesians 5:16, "Redeeming the time, because the days are evil."

Reflect

_____

_____

_____

_____

Relate

Remember the three Ds: dialogue daily, date weekly, and depart quarterly. Talk each day about each other's activities. Plan a special weekly date with your spouse and go to their favorite place; it may be a restaurant, shop, or the golf course, but plan it for just the two of you. At the beginning of each of the four seasons get away with your spouse even if it is just for one night. The observance of this routine will deposit unique treasures in your memory bank.

15

Never Insult Your Spouse

Nothing tears at the fabric of a marriage more than being insulted and ridiculed by one's own spouse. Name-calling, mocking, and belittling have no place in the building of a marriage in private or public.

My wife and I were chatting with a group of couples during a Hope for the Home conference, and one of the husbands made a comment regarding his wife's weight so that all could hear. Everyone could see the hurt and embarrassment on her face. On another occasion we were in the company of some friends when one of the wives began to belittle her husband for the type of work he did. He had left a secure nine-to-five job to pursue his dream vocation, which she felt was beneath his qualifications. Sometime later we found out they had divorced. He grew tired of being put down and compared to other men who were "making something of themselves." Later his dream turned into a very successful business.

Encouragement and reassurance are basic components in a strong marriage. Words of contempt, disrespect, and sarcasm will tear down a marriage. Words of acceptance, approval, and support will build one up.

Read

Proverbs 11:17, "The merciful man does good for his own soul, but he who is cruel troubles his own flesh."

Matthew 5:7, "Blessed are the merciful, for they shall obtain mercy."

Reflect

_____

_____

_____

_____

Relate

Make a list of words that hurt your feelings when spoken about you. Ask your spouse to do the same. Share your lists with each other. As you share the lists, file these words away in your "heart drive" and never use them again. Better yet, put these words in the Permanently Delete file.

16

Don't Be a Faultfinder

Lips of praise are the antidote for the lips of poison. Faultfinding is not a sign of strength, but a display of weakness. A husband or wife who is constantly pointing out the faults in their spouse does so because of their unwillingness to face the faults in their own life.

It is always easier to criticize others than to correct the imperfections in our own character. The harsh tongue reveals a blackened heart. The Bible tells us that as a little rudder can turn a great ship, so a little tongue can either bless or curse (James 3:4-10). Whoever said, "Sticks and stones may break my bones, but words will never hurt me," didn't understand the power of the spoken word. Cruel words are sharper than razors, and the damage they do leaves scars below the surface. Before marriage you could not say enough kind things to your future spouse, so why change the course of the ship after marriage? You have heard the expression, "I love you warts and all." There is much wisdom is this old proverb. Once you board the ship of marriage, there is no reason to abandon her or run her aground.

If words of commendation replaced words of condemnation, most husbands and wives would weather the storms that blow through a marriage. A wise man once said, "Fair words never hurt the tongue."

Everyone has faults. Everyone has imperfections. The eye that sees only the faults in others never sees itself. The one who is the first to condemn is often the last to forgive. We should think before we speak, as Shakespeare so aptly penned in *Hamlet*, "My words fly up, my thoughts remain below: words without thoughts never to heaven go." A spouse who dwells on the faults of their companion is like a cat concentrating on a mouse to the extent that it fails to see the dog standing behind it. Choose to focus on the strengths rather than the faults of your spouse. After all, you chose to ignore them while you were dating.

The opposite of faultfinding would be encouragement. Encouraging words are like sun to a flower, water to parched lips, wind to the sails, and joy to the heart. Instead of dwelling on the negative, accentuate the positive. It is just as easy to praise as it is to ridicule. The encourager brings gladness and joy to a marriage. The faultfinder brings sadness and pain. The encourager is like honey on the tongue. The faultfinder is like vinegar to the teeth. The encourager builds up. The faultfinder tears down.

Compassion, understanding, encouragement, cheerfulness, mercy, and sympathy are essential ingredients of a strong marriage. A husband and wife who master these virtues will not be guilty of faultfinding.

Read

Ecclesiastes 9:9, "Live joyfully with the wife whom you love all the days of your vain life."

Romans 12:10, "Be kindly affectionate to one another with brotherly love, in honor giving preference to one another."

Reflect

_____

_____

_____

_____

Relate

Make a list of the top ten things you like most about your spouse. Wrap this list in a box like a present and give it to them just before you go to bed tonight. It's a great way to end a day and start the next.

17

Remember Promises and Keep Them

The vows exchanged during the marriage ceremony are sacred. The vows made after the ceremony are equally important. Good intentions never substitute for following through. A promise broken is a memory made just as one that is kept. Spouses should not promise what they can not perform.

A spouse who does their best to keep their word is a person of character. Keeping promises develops strength in a marriage. This strength, like a fortified castle, will withstand the attacks from all the enemies that seek to surround a marriage and tear it down.

The husband or wife who can be counted on to keep their word is a spouse who can be counted on to defend and protect the marriage at all cost. I know there are unforeseen circumstances that can occur, but when these become the norm rather than the exception, then promises become fabrications that can unravel the marriage.

Promises delayed need not be denied. As soon as possible the purpose for which the promise was made should be fulfilled. This will restore the bonds of trust and respect. A promise, like truth, is a standard by which all things are judged. It is the foundation of a solid marriage, the measurement of character, the pattern of faithfulness, the banner of loyalty, and the rule of honesty. Spouses who keep their promises are likely to have children who will do the same.

Read

Numbers 30:2, "If a man vows a vow to the LORD, or swears an oath to bind himself by some agreement, he shall not break his word; he shall do according to all that proceeds out of his mouth."

Romans 4:21, "And being fully convinced that what He had promised He was also able to perform."

Reflect

_____

_____

_____

_____

Relate

Share with your spouse the value of keeping your word. In light of the scriptures given above discuss the importance of keeping a promise and the consequences of breaking a promise. When was the last time you failed to keep a promise? Have you asked forgiveness and have you made provisions to redeem the promise?

18

Never Compare Your Spouse to Others

If he was handsome enough for you to marry, then he is yours to keep. If you thought you were marrying the most beautiful girl in the world, then keep your eyes on her. Comparing your spouse to someone else will cause resentment, which will breed anger, which will drive you apart.

We live in a world where fantasy and fiction have replaced reality and responsibility. According to *Focus on the Family,* the number one addiction among men in the United States is Internet pornography, and women are not far behind. There are more than 4.2 million pornographic Web sites, which contain more than 372 million pages. Seventy percent of the women who are involved in Internet pornography keep their cyber activities secret, and 17 percent of the women in the United States struggle with pornography addiction. The statistics of children and teens visiting pornographic Web sites is appalling as well.

When our society is bombarded with sexual, sensual messages through print, radio, television, movies, concerts, CDs, iPods, and the Internet, is it any wonder that many husbands and wives end up comparing their spouses to others? These comparisons often lead to the dark alleys of addiction and affairs. It is for certain that one person can not meet all the needs of another, but turning to someone else or something else with impure and selfish motives is a sure way to end a marriage.

However, after the rice has been thrown and the honeymoon enjoyed, you need to keep yourself as attractive for your spouse as possible. What brought you together physically should keep you together.

A woman handed my wife a note after a session for husbands and wives. When we got back to the hotel she opened it and shared it with me. It read, "My knight in shining armor who once vowed his love so true, can no longer fit into his armor because instead of one of him now there's two." We got the picture. There is nothing attractive about a man who wears his belt under his belly or a woman who is a size eighteen trying to fit into a size eight.

Physical attractiveness is one outward way of saying "I love you," to your spouse. If you let yourself go, someone may come and go with your spouse.

Outer beauty is important, but inner beauty is a necessity for a strong and lasting marriage. There will be no need to compare your spouse to anyone else if the inner qualities of Christian character are developed and exhibited in daily living. It is not the gold and glamour of the world that give lasting beauty to a marriage, but the grace and goodness of the individuals in the marriage. Love and respect must be mutual. Just as a diseased tree dies a little at a time, so does a diseased marriage without these two essentials.

What is at the center always comes to the surface. Keep your eyes on each other, and your hearts centered in God's Word.

Read

Song of Solomon 4:1 (Solomon describing the Shulamite woman who would become his wife), "Behold, you are fair, my love! Behold, you are fair!"; 5:10 (the Shulamite woman describing Solomon), "My beloved is white and ruddy, chief among ten thousand."

1 John 2:16, "For all that is in the world—the lust of the flesh, the lust of the eyes, and the pride of life—is not of the Father but is of the world."

Reflect

_____

_____

_____

_____

Relate

As a couple read the eight chapters of the Song of Solomon together before going to bed tonight. Let the husband read the portions labeled "Beloved" and the wife read the sections labeled "The Shulamite." Discuss the love languages used by each to describe their feelings toward the other. You may want to read this book again on a regular basis.

19

Soft Words Reveal a Tender Heart

Jesus seldom raised his voice. When he did, it was under unusual circumstances, as when he cleared out the money changers in the temple and called out to his Father from the cross.

C. S. Lewis once said in a letter to a friend concerning words, "Isn't it funny the way some combinations of words can give you—almost apart from their meaning—a thrill like music?" This is so true in the language of love. As the early morning dew is to a tender plant, so are kind words to a tender heart. They never blister the tongue or the lips. Soft words will soften the soul and keep the marriage fresh. Cold words will freeze a relationship, and hot words will scorch it.

Words spoken without thought can not be retrieved once they leave the mouth. Better to learn the discipline of silence than to expose an unbridled tongue. Better to whisper and communicate your true feelings than to shout and conceal them. The language of dating should continue to be the mother tongue of marriage. This takes patience and work, but it will keep a marriage sweeter and take it farther down the road, making the journey much more enjoyable.

When God spoke to Elijah in the cave he did not shout at him, but rather the Bible says that he came to him in a still small voice. Save your shouting, screaming, screeching, and squawking for when the house is on fire.

Read

1 Kings 19:12, " . . . and after the earthquake a fire, but the LORD was not in the fire; and after the fire a still small voice."

Galatians 5:22–23, "But the fruit of the Spirit is love, joy, peace, longsuffering, kindness, goodness, faithfulness, gentleness, self-control. Against such there is no law."

Reflect

_____

_____

_____

_____

Relate

Make a list of ten love words that describe your spouse, and ask your spouse to do the same for you. Share these words with each other either before going off to work or before going to bed. Why not call your spouse sometime today and use one of those love words? It will make coming home tonight something special.

20

Include Your Spouse in Conversations with Others

No one wants to feel left out. Being ignored not only hurts, it lowers self-esteem and builds up anger.

I have often observed a husband talking to other men while standing with his wife and totally ignoring her. I have also seen the opposite take place—a woman chatting away with friends while her husband stood by alone and disregarded. Feeling like the hole in a donut makes a spouse feel absolutely unnecessary.

The movie *Castaway* featured a man who was stranded on a deserted island for a number of years. His need for conversation and company was so great he talked daily with his "friend" Wilson, who was a volleyball. Don't make your spouse start talking to inanimate objects!

Be sure you make your spouse feel included in your conversations whenever the two of you are out with others. It will not only strengthen your marriage, it will also deepen your friendship.

Remember your dating days? You did not want to go anywhere without your honey. And when you two were at a party or some other event, you would never think of neglecting them. So, why do it now? Including your spouse is another way of saying "I love you," whether you are sitting in church, standing in line at a reception, or walking through the mall.

Read

Amos 3:3, "Can two walk together, unless they are agreed?"

Colossians 4:6, "Let your speech always be with grace, seasoned with salt, that you may know how you ought to answer each one."

Reflect

_____

_____

_____

_____

Relate

Share with each other the last time you felt left out or neglected. Talk about your feelings on that occasion and how you dealt with them. Make a promise never to intentionally overlook or be inattentive to each other again.

21

Include Your Spouse in the Events of the Day

If you work outside the home, then 90 percent of your conversation is expended by the time you pull into the driveway. If you are a stay-at-home spouse or work out of your home, then you still have 90 percent of your conversation to share when your spouse arrives from having been out in the workplace. Either way, it is important to sit down together and share the events of the day. Even if it seems routine, it is good to look into each other's eyes and talk and listen.

Some professions are more technical and stressful than others, and as a result a spouse may be reluctant to open up and share. I know from counseling with individuals in law enforcement that they are often involved with circumstances that do not make for pleasant dinner conversation. You do not have to give all the details. Just talking through some of the events of the day will help both of you unwind and make the rest of the evening more relaxing.

Exchanging the highlights of the day can lead to exchanging more than conversation when the lights are dimmed at night. Showing genuine interest in your spouse's day makes homecoming a great deal more enjoyable for both of you. After all, if you are not willing to listen and share with your spouse, someone else is. There are always those with open ears and hidden motives.

Read

Proverbs 15:31, "The ear that hears the reproof of life will abide among the wise."

Hebrews 2:1, "Therefore we must give the more earnest heed to the things we have heard, lest we drift away."

Reflect

_____

_____

_____

_____

Relate

As a couple, share something with one another that happened at work today that was out of the ordinary. Talk about the things or people at work that cause you the most stress. Listen carefully and offer encouragement without "preaching" to the other what you would do if you were in their place. More often than not, spouses just need the person they care about the most to really listen to their highs and lows of the day. Going to bed having shared the events of the day makes getting up the next morning a great deal easier.

22

Practice Good Manners

Regardless of what may or may not be the mores of the times, good manners and proper etiquette never go out of style. There is no substitute for their presence and no excuse for their absence. Treating your spouse with a keen sense of courtesy reflects not only the feelings you have toward them, but is a reflection of your own self-image.

Good manners begin at home. Your behavior toward your spouse is permanently stamped on the hearts of your children. They will likely exhibit and expect the same conduct in their marriage unless what they have witnessed has been most cruel; in which case they may end up expecting perfection or accepting abuse. A well-timed "Thank you," a bouquet of flowers, or an unexpected compliment is sweeter to the heart than honey to the lips.

Husbands, giving your wife undivided attention, opening the door for her, pulling out her chair at the dinner table, and helping her clear the table, which we husbands pay others to do at fancy restaurants, is a low-cost way of enriching your marriage.

Wives, the practice of good manners is not reserved just for the male species. Most husbands appreciate a clean home, unless you married a Neanderthal, in which case I suggest you move into a cave. Most husbands notice the clean clothes that their wives have taken the time to fold. Most husbands like to hear their wives compliment their work. It's the little things that add up to big dividends.

Being a gentleman and a gentlewoman is more than bloodline and breeding. Your ancestors may have come over on the *Mayflower*, but your good manners come from within. You may have inherited a fortune, and be bankrupt when it comes to the practice of civility.

Very simply, a gentleman or gentlewoman is someone who is gentle. Good manners and gentleness are not a sign of weakness, but rather the opposite. It takes a strong individual to be courteous, friendly, polite, respectful, and self-controlled. These traits in a husband and wife are the building blocks of a lasting marriage. When lived out in front of your children, these qualities become the fabric of the legacy you pass down.

Good manners, like fine porcelain, must be painted before they are glazed. Like a rare oriental rug with the back as beautiful as the front, so it is with the practice of good manners. A gentle husband and gentle wife are the same in the home and out of the home.

Good manners are but the shadows of godly virtues. If each of you strive to become to your spouse and children what you strive to appear to them to be, then your actions and words will be the same. A marriage that starts with manners should end with manners. The attention and respect you paid to each other during the dating days should be the standard during the marriage marathon.

Read

Genesis 2:24, "Therefore a man shall leave his father and mother and be joined to his wife, and they shall become one flesh."

James 3:13, "Who is wise and understanding among you? Let him show by good conduct [manners] that his works are done in the meekness of wisdom."

Reflect

_____

_____

_____

_____

Relate

Share with your spouse the qualities about them you admire the most. Talk about ways in which each of you can practice good manners toward the other. Then each time this is done put it in your "love investment" folder and very soon the dividends will start pouring in.

23

Show Affection toward Each Other in Public

Walking hand in hand is not reserved for dating couples and newlyweds. How often do you see a husband and wife exhibiting appropriate affection in public? It is a testimony to those around them that they are still in love and that romance is not reserved for the young. A single tender kiss on the cheek can say more than a hundred words. A couple gazing into each other's eyes, whether over a candlelit dinner or a hot dog at the ball game, speaks volumes to those who may be watching.

With all the immoral, perverted, and unholy displays of affection in public and in the media, it is refreshing to see a couple, or a family, show their love and devotion to each other. Touching is unspoken communication. A hug, a squeeze, an embrace are all ways that fathers and mothers can teach their children healthy expressions of affection while at the same time reaffirming their love for each other. After all, little boys and girls watch their parents and learn from them how to express their feelings and actions toward the opposite sex. A major reason for the unnatural sexual habits and practices of many of our teens is that they have never seen natural affection displayed in their homes.

What you watch, your children will watch. What you do, they will do. The way you treat your spouse is probably the way they will treat theirs.

Read

Song of Solomon 8:5, "Who is this coming up from the wilderness, leaning upon her beloved?"

Ephesians 5:2, "And walk in love, as Christ also has loved us and given Himself for us, an offering and a sacrifice to God for a sweet-smelling aroma."

Reflect

_____

_____

_____

_____

Relate

Share with your spouse some of the ways you two can express wholesome public affection for each other. Observe other couples at restaurants, shopping malls, and various public places and see how few express any affection or communication of any type. If your children are still at home, ask them how they know that Dad and Mom love each other. You may be surprised at their answers.

24

Be Open to Giving and Receiving Loving Counsel

It is a wise and mature individual who listens to the compassionate counsel of their spouse. So important is tender, compassionate counsel that God made Counselor one of the great names of His Son (Isa. 9:6). No one knows you better than your mate. Once a weakness is pointed out, it is a sign of strength and positive self-image to correct that flaw. The greatest trust between a husband and wife is the trust of giving and receiving counsel.

When constructive criticism is given, it should not come in like a hurricane, blowing down everything in its path. Loving counsel is meant to cherish, refresh, and encourage. It should come down like the evening dew on the grass or like gentle snowflakes that land one at a time. The softer it falls, the longer it remains. The longer it remains, the deeper it sinks into the mind and heart.

Timing is everything when pointing out a weakness or imperfection. Never give advice or counsel when your spouse is already feeling defeated and deflated. This is the time for encouragement. Offering personal counsel that may open a wound requires the skill of a surgeon and the sensitivity of a diamond cutter.

Desiring what is best for the one you love is the

only motive for wanting to correct their behavior. This type of counsel resembles stain remover; it not only removes the spots, but it rubs off when it is dry. After the counsel is given, leave it in the hands of God and the heart of your spouse. There is no need to repeat the process; it will insure the opposite effect of the desired results.

Read

Proverbs 12:15, "The way of a fool is right in his own eyes, but he who heeds counsel is wise."

James 4:17, "Therefore, to him who knows to do good and does not do it, to him it is sin."

Reflect

_____

_____

_____

_____

Relate

When is the best time to share constructive remarks with your spouse? What tone of voice do you use when giving counsel to your spouse? How do you react when your spouse points out an area in your character that needs adjusting? Make a list of the areas in your life that need to be strengthened and ask your spouse to do the same. Compare lists and offer to hold each other accountable.

25

Respect Each Other in Sexual Matters

As we have noted, most husbands and wives are different. Husbands are visual. Wives are emotive. Husbands are instantaneous. Wives are reflective. Husbands gulp. Wives sip. Husbands grunt. Wives chat. Husbands sweat. Wives dew. Husbands are Stone Age. Wives are Renaissance. Husbands are little boys in older bodies. Wives are little girls who never grow old. Husbands are controlling. Wives are diplomats. Whether these description match you and your spouse or not, you will agree that there is a difference between husbands and wives. Thank the Lord for that difference.

However, both husbands and wives are sexual in nature. It is this area of married life where the partners either share the deepest form of communication on a mutually enjoyable level or find that what is pleasurable for one may be embarrassing for the other.

Our society is bombarded with sexual images 24/7. According to *Focus on the Family,* the number one addiction at the present among men in the United States is Internet pornography. It is growing in interest among women as well. Men get caught up in a fantasy world where the very objects of their desires are most often air-brushed desperate models whose personal lives are as false as their implants. Women who turn to Internet pornography visit chat rooms that often lead to bedrooms in some other city or state.

The act of sexual intimacy was designed by God to be one of the greatest pleasures a couple can experience. Intimacy is like an equilateral triangle. Its three sides are sexual, sensual, and spiritual. Sexual is the physical side. Sensual is the emotional side. Spiritual is the foundational side. If all three sides are not in proportion to each other, then the intimate part of the marriage becomes one-sided and out of balance.

If you wish to become a great lover to your spouse, then an understanding of the three sides of intimacy is vital. By the way, a "scientific survey" for husbands revealed that if a husband is balding in front, it proves he is a great lover. If he is balding in back, he is a great thinker. If he is balding all over, he just thinks he is a great lover.

In the context of a loving marriage, sexual intimacy is an expression of commitment and trust at the deepest level. It exposes the body, mind, and spirit. This is one reason God's Word condemns adultery. It was God who created the sex drive. It was God who created the first man and woman. It was God who said, "For this reason a man shall leave his father and mother and be joined to his wife, and the two shall become one flesh" (Matt. 19:5). It was Jesus, God's Son, who said, "Therefore what God has joined together, let not man separate" (v. 6).

One of the most significant ways a married couple can honor God is to honor their vows. Great sex in a marriage requires openness, honesty, and trust without violating either God's laws or your spouse.

Read

Song of Solomon 1:2; 7:1 (the woman speaks) "Let him kiss me with the kisses of his mouth—for your love is better than wine." (Solomon speaks) "How beautiful are your feet in sandals, O prince's daughter! The curves of your thighs are like jewels, the work of the hands of a skillful workman."

1 Corinthians 7:2-3, "Nevertheless, because of sexual immorality, let each man have his own wife, and let each woman have her own husband. Let the husband render to his wife the affection due her, and likewise also the wife to her husband."

Reflect

_____

_____

_____

_____

Relate

Discuss the triangle model of intimacy with your spouse. Are there any adjustments that need to be made in your sexual relationship? If so, share them with one other.

26

Prepare for Sexual Intimacy

Preparation for expressing physical intimacy enhances the experience. One reason husbands and wives get involved in extramarital affairs is that one or the other approaches lovemaking with about as much interest as taking out the garbage. It's just something you have to do. This attitude will either shut down your lovemaking altogether or drive your spouse into the bed of another. A husband or wife who has no desire for sex is in need of help from a qualified counselor. A celibate marriage is an oxymoron unless it is because of medical reasons or getting married after you are 100.

Two of the greatest areas of conflict in marriage are sexual dissatisfaction and financial bondage. The bedroom should not be used as a "DMZ" (Demilitarized Zone) between marital battles. Calling a truce and meeting in the bedroom only to continue the war afterward will soon cause both sides to go down in defeat. The credit card and checkbook are not to be used as "WMDs" (Weapons of Marital Destruction). This will create a chasm that neither side can cross. In preparation for those special times together, beware of the sexual spoilers.

First as already mentioned is the Internet. Every computer in your home should be in full view for every family member to see. Secret passwords should not be allowed for personal use. This keeps everyone accountable.

Second is work. Do not bring it into the bedroom. A husband and father who leaves home at 6:30 each morning and does not return until 6:30 each evening will have little time for his wife and children. The same applies to the wife and mother who works outside the home. Too much work leaves you exhausted and your spouse open to the temptation of finding someone who will give them the attention they need. The best way to spell love to your spouse is not "overtime" but "personal time."

The third spoiler is children. Children are demanding. Their whole world revolves around them. When they begin to dominate the time you need to spend with your spouse, then a family council is in order. If you allow your children to sleep in bed with you and they are older than three weeks, then you are headed for big trouble. If you use your child or children as an excuse not to enjoy intimacy with your spouse, you are not only driving a wedge between you two, you are building a barrier between your spouse and the children. I have often heard from a neglected spouse, "Our marriage was fine before the kids came." Don't give reason for this to be said concerning your marriage.

Sexual spoilers are only one reason why husbands and wives find themselves sleeping with someone else. There are at least five other marriage spoilers that can crash a marriage. First is grief. So often when tragedy strikes a marriage in the form of the death of a child or some serious illness, the spouses rather than clinging to each other retreat into their own little worlds and thus close out the other. If communication is not established and feelings shared, the death of the marriage may follow as one of the spouses finds comfort in the arms of another.

Second is separation. When couples are apart for long periods of time the temptation to fill that void with someone else may be more than a spouse can endure. A marriage can be headed for trouble when the vocation of a spouse requires more nights on the road than at home. Your first priority is your marriage, then your children, and finally your job.

Third is isolation. When you spend a great deal of time alone with the opposite sex you are setting your marriage up for a fall. It may be at work, the fitness center, or even in the church choir, but isolation with the opposite sex is not healthy for the marriage.

Fourth is success. I have met many husbands who are too successful for their own good. The companion of their youth has been discarded for a new model, and they regress to younger days that are only making them older but not wiser. They think they need a cute little thing hanging on their arm, a Rolex on their wrist, a gold card in their wallet, and a new set of wheels in the garage. They belong to every elite club in town and serve on the most prestigious boards in the community. They have become legends in their own minds.

Fifth is friendship. Often when a spouse becomes involved in an affair, it is with someone who is in their inner circle of friends. How many times have you heard about someone getting divorced because their spouse was sleeping with the other's best friend? The saying that the husband or wife is the last to know is so true. Friendships are great so long as they do not interfere with or take the place of your best friend, namely your spouse.

It has been reported that husbands think about sex thirty-three times a day while their wives think about sex once a day—and that is when their husbands remind them. Affection means different things to a wife and a husband. It is a wise couple who understands this and seeks to voluntarily meet each other's needs with enthusiasm and creativity. Someone has said that a married couple can't live on sex, but it is a great way to go. Prepare for and anticipate those intimate times with your spouse, but remember the three sides of intimacy as discussed in the previous chapter. You will find that sex alone leads not to a lasting marriage but to a fragmented relationship.

Read

Song of Solomon 4:1, 9, 11, "Behold, you are fair, my love! Behold, you are fair! . . . You have ravished my heart. . . . Your lips, O my spouse, drip as the honeycomb."

Hebrews 13:4, "Marriage is honorable among all, and the bed undefiled; but fornicators and adulterers God will judge."

Reflect

_____

_____

_____

_____

Relate

Read the entire fourth chapter of the Song of Solomon together and discuss the love language used in it. Then light the candles and . . . if you have children make sure they are in bed fast asleep.

27

Celebrate Special Events

Whether your spouse admits it or not, everyone likes to be remembered on special occasions like birthdays and anniversaries. It is not the expense involved, but the expression that is important.

Take the time to send a card and flowers. Take the time to select a special gift. Take the time for a nice dinner with just the two of you. If possible, take the time for a weekend getaway. This speaks volumes to the one you love. This is time well spent. It is an affirmation of the past and an investment in the future.

If you have to program your computer to remind you of an upcoming anniversary or special occasion, then do so. Planning a special event together will give both of you something to look forward to, and as the time approaches the excitement and anticipation will build. If you are in the habit of taking an annual vacation, then give that tradition priority in your schedule each year.

Our friends in Scotland plan a year or two in advance for their holidays. It is something the entire family enjoys. A wife of forty-five years told my wife that in her years of marriage she and her husband had a formula that they had always honored. They dialogue daily; date weekly, and depart quarterly to some special place for the weekend. This has served them well and has been a source of renewal and strength for their marriage.

If you do not take the time for special events, the "wish I hads" will replace the "glad I dids."

Read

Psalm 118:24, "This is the day which the LORD has made; we will rejoice and be glad in it."

2 Corinthians 9:7, "So let each one give as he purposes in his heart, not grudgingly or of necessity; for God loves a cheerful giver."

Reflect

_____

_____

_____

_____

Relate

Plan an unexpected date with your spouse and spend that time sharing some of the greatest memories you two have made over the months and years. Do not dwell on the negative, only the positive. Make a vow to each other that you will create your own special events on a regular basis.

28

Be an Encourager to One Another

Each of you should be your spouse's greatest cheer-leader. Nothing helps you reach your full potential like someone standing on the sidelines cheering you on. And that someone should be your spouse. Never be afraid that they will eclipse you and leave you behind.

A solid marriage is not built on fear, but trust and encouragement. When you and your spouse inspire one another, you are strengthening the foundation of your marriage. Anyone can criticize, castigate, and condemn. A loving spouse will applaud, affirm, and approve.

A note of caution is called for at this point. As the two of you stretch and reach those dreams, always remember the one who stood beside you until the finish line was crossed. The encourager in a marriage also needs to be lifted up.

Often I have talked with a husband or a wife who was left in the dust after the other spouse had received their advanced degree or big promotion. One such husband told me that in the middle of a football game his wife informed him she had received a promotion with the bank that required her to move to another city. She had accepted the promotion without sharing the news with him. When he asked what she expected him to do about his job, she told him to keep it because she was going alone to her new position.

Husbands and wives who start well will finish well

so long as each knows when to cheer and when to run. A lasting marriage is a marathon, not a sprint.

Read

Jeremiah 9:23-24, "Thus says the LORD: 'Let not the wise man glory in his wisdom, let not the mighty man glory in his might, nor let the rich man glory in his riches; but let him who glories glory in this, that he understands and knows Me, that I am the LORD, exercising loving kindness, judgment, and righteousness in the earth. For in these I delight,' says the LORD."

1 Thessalonians 5:11, "Therefore comfort each other and edify one another, just as you also are doing."

Reflect

_____

_____

_____

_____

Relate

Share areas in your life where you need to be encouraged. Become a cheerleader for each other.

29

Avoid Irritating Comments

Everyone has a built-in set of "hot buttons." Pushing those buttons is a guarantee we are either deliberating trying to hurt someone, or we are retaliating for a hurt inflicted on our spirit. Either way, words can be more destructive than any man-made weapon.

The Bible says that the tongue is untamable; with our words we bless, and with our words we curse (James 3:3-9). Picking a verbal fight is a sign of both immaturity and low self-esteem. Rather than using creative expressions to communicate our feelings, we often resort to childish behavior and destructive words. What would seldom happen during the dating days often becomes commonplace in a marriage.

Let me suggest some Spouse Steaming Statements to avoid: "I told you so"; "You can't expect any better because you were raised that way"; "You should have"; "You never"; "You always"; "Next time maybe you will listen to me"; "You did exactly as I expected you to do"; "If you don't know, I'm not going to tell you"; "Are you going to wear that?"; "Why don't you just stop and ask for directions?"; "I was never late until I married you"; "Don't use 'big' and 'but' in the same sentence"; "It's your tone of voice"; "I wish you would quit flipping the channel changer"; and, "Call my mother and ask her how to cook it."

You can come up with your own list, and after you do, throw it away.

Read

Proverbs 15:2, "The tongue of the wise uses knowledge rightly, but the mouth of fools pours forth foolishness."

Ephesians 4:31, "Let all bitterness, wrath, anger, clamor, and evil speaking be put away from you, with all malice."

Reflect

_____

_____

_____

_____

Relate

As suggested above, make a list of "hot button" words and phrases that you do not like to hear. Share them with your spouse and have them make their own list. After you have read them together, promise each other you will make an effort not to use these words in future conversations. When you do, you owe the other one a dinner at the restaurant of their choice.

30

Defend Your Spouse

Defending your spouse is a sure sign of your devotion. Do not allow anyone to insult, dishonor, or offend your spouse. Someone of the opposite sex with hidden motives and a loose tongue can plant seeds of destruction in a marriage. Any comments of this nature must be uprooted immediately. Your best friend should be your spouse, and one characteristic of best friends is that they protect and defend that friendship at all costs.

If someone in your circle of friends makes any degrading or demeaning remark about your spouse, let them know in no uncertain terms that you do not appreciate such comments, nor will you tolerate them.

The mustard seeds of doubt can be planted by the enemy posing as your friend. Most often if someone attacks your spouse, it is done out of envy. Satan attacked Adam through Eve because he had lost his position of guardian of God's throne in heaven and was confined to dealing with mere mortals. His nature has always been to make man rebel first against God and second against those he loves. As Jesus so accurately stated concerning Satan, "He was a murderer from the beginning, and does not stand in the truth, because there is no truth in him. When he speaks a lie, he speaks from his own resources, for he is a liar and the father of it" (John 8:44). Evil people will try to lessen what they are unwilling to imitate. So, if someone disguised as your friend attempts to belittle your spouse or create doubt in your mind as to their faithfulness or questions their character, cut off that friendship as you would the head of a snake. As a nation is strengthened by a strong defense, so is a marriage.

What people protect the most they love the most. There is no greater gift that deserves more protection than the gift of a faithful spouse. They stand by us when others desert us. They encourage us when others deject us. They inspire us when others drain us. They comfort us when others reject us. They laugh with us when others laugh at us. They accept us when others ridicule us. They calm us when others trouble us. They preserve us when others attack us. This kind of relationship deserves to be defended, protected, and safeguarded at all cost. As you were the guardian of your love before marriage so you must continue to be afterward.

Read

Nehemiah 4:14, "And I looked, and arose and said to the nobles, to the leaders, and to the rest of the people, 'Do not be afraid of them. Remember the Lord, great and awesome, and fight for your brethren, your sons, your daughters, your wives, and your houses.'"

Ephesians 5:33, "Nevertheless let each one of you in particular so love his own wife as himself, and let the wife see that she respects her husband."

Reflect

_____

_____

_____

_____

Relate

Share with each other some occasion when you defended one another from either the remarks or the actions of others. How does it make each of you feel to know that your spouse is always there to protect you?

31

Be Considerate of Sensitive Areas of Your Spouse's Life

The use of backhanded, cruel remarks thinly disguised as humor with the intention of hurting your spouse has no place in a marriage. As stated in the previous suggestion, not only are you to defend your spouse from the verbal attacks of others, you are to make doubly sure that no discourteous and disrespectful statements come from your mouth aimed at your mate. I have seen wives brought to tears by insensitive, crude, ill-mannered, barbaric, obnoxious husbands using distorted humor to inflict emotional pain. This will most certainly create cracks in the foundation and eventually bring the whole marriage down with it.

All people have something about themselves they would like to change. Even Adam and Eve, the first husband and wife, had flaws; neither one had a belly button. Pointing out your spouse's imperfections only underscores your own.

Because of our sexually saturated society and the 24/7 emphasis on remaining young forever, true beauty has been replaced by a nip and a tuck. True beauty does not fade with time. It is not dependent on the physical features, but on the spiritual form that lies beneath the surface.

A truly beautiful wife is one whose outward appearance is surpassed by her inner qualities. Flowers will fade. Grass will wither. Dew will evaporate. Leaves will fall. But true inner beauty will last forever. A pretty woman will please the eye; a beautiful woman will please the heart. The one is a jewel; the other a treasure.

Husband, you need to understand that when your wife begins to lose the charms of her youth, she is the first to notice. She begins to wonder if she is still attractive and appealing. It is at this time you must reassure her that the love that brought you together is stronger than ever and that neither wrinkles nor gray hair can weaken the vows when the bloom is no longer on the rose. After all, it is not only the wife who enters the fall and winter years of life. Time can not erase what it can not destroy. So, never let remarks leave your mouth to cause the petals of love to fall. Be sensitive to both the inner and outer characteristics of your spouse.

Read

Proverbs 14:13, "Even in laughter the heart may sorrow, and the end of mirth may be grief."

James 3:8, "But no man can tame the tongue. It is an unruly evil, full of deadly poison."

Reflect

_____

_____

_____

_____

Relate

Do you use humor to hurt your spouse? If so, then you need to apologize and ask forgiveness. Share the things that attracted you two to each other in the first place. Continue to compliment one other on these strengths and do not dwell on the weaknesses. However, if you have purposely neglected your strengths, it will weaken your marriage. Longevity is no excuse for laziness.

32

Never Pick a Fight

Picking a fight is a sure sign of immaturity and insecurity. If you are the type of individual who always has to win, guess what, you are a natural-born loser. No one is always right. No one is always wrong. I once had a secretary who remembered as a little girl her father and mother getting into a verbal fight. She said it was clearly her father's fault, but he would not speak to her mother until she apologized. This father left a lasting imprint on his daughter's heart. Rather than embracing in the arms of love, many couples are constantly issuing a call to arms. Instead of loving lips speaking words of encouragement, too many husbands and wives are in the cannon's mouth firing round after round of explosive remarks. And all too often verbal abuse is followed by physical abuse. The adage that says "Sticks and stones may break my bones, but words will never hurt me" is a lie. Many spouses have shared that words spoken in anger are more painful than physical mistreatment. Physical abuse may leave scars on the skin, but verbal abuse scars the heart.

There are several types of abuse one spouse may inflict on the other: (1) Physical, which may consist of just one incident, or it may happen repeatedly. (2) Sexual, which includes all forms of sexual assault, sexual harassment, or sexual exploitation. (3) Emotional, which includes verbal attacks, such as yelling, screaming, and name-calling. Criticism, verbal threats, social isolation, intimidation, or exploitation to dominate another person are other forms. (4) Economic, which includes stealing from or defrauding a partner. Withholding money that is necessary to buy food or medical treatment, manipulating or exploiting a person for financial gain, denying them access to financial resources, or preventing them from working (or controlling their choice of occupation) are also forms of economic abuse. (5) Spiritual, which includes using a person's religious or spiritual beliefs to manipulate, dominate, or control them. It may include preventing someone from engaging in spiritual or religious practices, or ridiculing their beliefs.

Most spousal abuse is directed toward the wife. It is as common in rural areas as in cities. It is common in high-income families as well as low-income families. It spans all ages, races, and nationalities. Wife abuse rarely happens as a one-time occurrence. Wife abuse frequently occurs after hours between 5:00 P.M. and 7:00 A.M. and on weekends. Wife abuse always happens in private places. Wife abuse often occurs during pregnancy and often starts during a first pregnancy. It can result in minor injuries or, in extreme cases, death.

Husbands who abuse their wives often have low self-esteem and poor communication skills, are impulsive in their actions, have a strong need to control, and have a tendency to blame the victim and other factors for their actions. The same characteristics apply to a wife who abuses her husband.

There is no room in a marriage for anger to be the

common expression of communication. If either you or your spouse are dealing with the issue of spousal abuse, please seek professional counsel immediately. Not only will it destroy your marriage, it can destroy the future marriages of your children. You can call your pastor, your physician, or a local law enforcement officer. Too many wives never report abuse for fear of being left without any means of financial support for themselves and the children. If this should be your situation, there is help available, and I urge you to seek it today.

Read

Proverbs 15:1, "A soft answer turns away wrath, but a harsh word stirs up anger."

Ephesians 5:29, "For no one ever hated his own flesh, but nourishes and cherishes it, just as the Lord does the church."

Reflect

_____

_____

_____

_____

Relate

Share with your spouse your views and feelings regarding the five types of spousal abuse listed above. If any of these apply to either of you, talk about it in an open, honest manner. Admitting an area of weakness is the first step in strengthening your marriage.

33

Express Gratitude

You have heard the expression, "Have an attitude of gratitude." This works well in a marriage. All the polite, courteous things you said to each other during your dating days need to be said during the wedding years. Good words warm the heart like sunbeams warm the body. "Thank you," "How may I help you?" "I really appreciate that," are essential in the vocabulary of any marriage that seeks to be continually strengthened.

The language of gratitude is picked up by children. When they hear various expressions of gratitude coming from their parents, it will be natural for them to follow suit. Good manners are more caught than taught. Gratitude also has a silent language which husbands and wives can master. The sweet smile, the gracious glance, the tender touch, and the peaceful presence of the other are ways of communicating volumes of kindness without speaking a word.

A grateful heart not only enriches beauty, it is an excellent substitute when the physical charms begin to fade. When time has left its etchings on the face, the inner grace of elegance and good manners will more than substitute for the loss of the outer ornaments of appearance and cosmetics. Physical beauty is a gift from God to be enjoyed for a season. A grateful heart is a gem of eternal beauty. Certainly you should always stay as attractive as possible for your spouse. Neglecting yourself physically is a sure sign of apathy and an undisciplined lifestyle. If you let yourself go, then someone may come along and go with your spouse. However, beneath the surface there must be springs of kindness, forgiveness, mercy, compassion, tenderness, and friendship that flow like an artesian well into a bottomless pool of gratitude.

All of the small day-to-day things that a wife does for her husband and children should not be taken for granted. The hard work and material goods provided by the husband for his wife and children are deserving of expressions of gratitude as well. Ingratitude springs from a heart of pride that expects to be served, but is never willing to serve.

When Jesus healed the ten lepers, only one returned to express gratitude (Luke 17:11-19). This kind of ungratefulness in a marriage will do more harm than the leprosy itself. It is a wise and caring spouse who practices expressions of gratitude whenever the occasion arises.

Read

Proverbs 31:30, "Charm is deceitful and beauty is vain, but a woman who fears the LORD, she shall be praised."

Ephesians 5:20, "Giving thanks always for all things to God the Father in the name of our Lord Jesus Christ."

Reflect

_____

_____

_____

_____

Relate

Before you go to bed tonight share with your spouse some of the small things they do for which you are grateful. Discuss ways that expressions of gratitude can be taught to your children. Offer a prayer of thanks to God for the blessings He has given you, your spouse, and your family.

34

Be a Person of Integrity

I have a friend who is in charge of the vault in a very large bank. Every day he watches people either deposit valuables in their lockboxes or withdraw them for various reasons. He said some individuals just turn their boxes upside down on the table with thousands of dollars pouring out and enough jewelry to turn the Pirates of the Caribbean green with envy.

People can be rich with the trappings of this world and be impoverished in the area of character and integrity. A great marriage is not built on the things stored in a lockbox, draped around the shoulders, or parked in a garage. A great marriage is built on the intangibles of life: character, honesty, and integrity.

Integrity is the foundation of all that is high and noble. It flows in the deep clear waters, not in the murky shallows. It associates with that which is superior and does not keep company with that which is inferior. Integrity is a character trait of those who are honest, sound from center to circumference; those who condemn wrong in friend or foe alike, and especially in themselves; those who are devout in their dealings, earnest in their expectations, genuine in their relations, and pure in their motives.

Husbands and wives of integrity stand for the right even if they stand alone. They neither brag nor run.

They have courage without shouting about it and strength without abusing it. They know their convictions and speak them without fear of rejection. They know their positions of authority and fill them without compromise. They are trustworthy, and therefore they can be trusted.

Integrity is not developed suddenly. It is like the mighty oak that starts from a tiny acorn, but given time stands above all the other trees of the forest. How tragic when those who start out with a solid marriage begin to listen to the seductive sirens of the world and shipwreck on the rocks of pride, immorality, and greed. There is a high price to be paid for low living.

Just as an icicle is lengthened one drop at a time, so is integrity in the seasons of marriage. If the water that forms the icicle remains clear, then it sparkles in the winter sun and is a source of wonder. If the water is muddy, then the icicle becomes an object of repulsion. We as husbands and wives must develop our integrity drop by drop, day by day. Like the icicle, if our lives are pure and right, our marriages will be bright and clear. However, if we say one thing and practice another, our marriages will become tainted and polluted.

The price of integrity is a righteous life that will strengthen your marriage.

Read

Proverbs 20:7, "The righteous man walks in his integrity; his children are blessed after him."

Philippians 4:8, "Finally, brethren, whatever things are true, whatever things are noble, whatever things are just, whatever things are pure, whatever things are lovely, whatever things are of good report, if there is any virtue and if there is anything praiseworthy—meditate on these things."

Reflect

_____

_____

_____

_____

Relate

Share with your spouse what the word "integrity" means to you. How is it demonstrated in your marriage, family, and work? Reread the scriptures above and discuss them with each other.

35

Maintain Your Marriage While Working Your Work

We have become a nation where many a husband and wife stay married to their work while divorcing their spouse. As one CEO stated, "I spent my entire career climbing the ladder of success, and when I reached the top, I realized that my ladder was leaning against the wrong wall." The lie that it may be necessary to sacrifice marriage and family to be successful has claimed many a victim.

At the conclusion of one of our Hope for the Home conferences, a gentleman approached me and asked if he could have a minute of my time. As we stepped outside into the hot, humid August night he related to me his story. He said that as a young pastor he modeled his ministry after men who led the megachurches. His ambition was to become the pastor of the largest church in his state. In just a few short years he had achieved his goal. He was well known among his peers and was a much-sought-after speaker in the major conferences and conventions of his denomination.

Then after telling me these things, he stopped talking. Tears began to fall from his eyes and splatter on the steaming asphalt pavement. He said that one night he came home from one of the high-powered committee meetings at church, and as he entered the kitchen a large handwritten note on the refrigerator froze him in his tracks. It simply said, "I am gone and have taken the children, and you will never miss us."

Looking at me with the appearance of a broken man, he said, "And they never came back."

A man may be a pastor and fail to pastor his own family. He may listen to the voices of other wives in his church and never hear the cry of his own wife. He may seek to save other children and lose his own.

Husbands and wives often prostitute their marriages to reach an elusive position of prominence. This leaves a huge hole in the resume of life. Prostitution is far more than a physical act. It corrodes the conscience. It corrupts the character. It disgraces and destroys the body. It eliminates the estate. It ends in evil conduct. It fragments families. It hardens the heart. It ruins reputations. It wakens the wrath of God.

Selling yourself to your job robs your spouse of the person they married. Why do you work sixty, seventy, eighty hours a week? The answer is simple. You have chosen covetousness over contentment and splash over simplicity. You buy things you do not really want to impress people you do not really like. You try to keep up with the Joneses when they have no idea where they are going. The enjoyment of your spouse's company is replaced by the fellowship of your coworkers at the company. Instead of hugging your spouse, you end up holding your PC. All this is done in the name of working to enrich your marriage when in reality it is only leading to marital bankruptcy.

Read

Proverbs 13:7, "There is one who makes himself rich, yet has nothing; and one who makes himself poor, yet has great riches."

Mark 8:36, "For what will it profit a man if he gains the whole world, and loses his own soul? Or, what will a man give in exchange for his soul?"

Reflect

_____

_____

_____

_____

Relate

Before going to bed tonight discuss with your spouse what, if any, stress is being created by the hours you put in at work. Is there time for intimacy? Is there time for your children? Is there time for your own personal growth? What are the real reasons for working such long hours?

36

Practice Your Priorities

The adage "Practice makes perfect" is wrong. It leads you to believe that with enough practice you will always be perfect in your performance. Practice makes perfect practice. Only on rare occasions will you score a perfect 10. However, you will never score 10 if you have not practiced.

In sports, no individual or team wins every game or tournament. But no individual or team will ever win any game or tournament without much practice.

If this principle applies to sports, it certainly applies to marriage. You two got together for special dates before children, so keep those special dates after children. Your children won't forget you while you are at a dinner and a movie together. If they do, just know you have children with short attention spans. Hang a picture of you two around their necks while you are on that date. Don't let your children come between you.

Young couples often find that dream of spending twenty-four hours together every day turning into trying to squeeze in an hour a day to be together. With different jobs at different times along with new financial obligations and demands you must continue to practice your priorities.

It is only natural that some priorities must be rearranged from time to time, but keep first things first. During the first few years of marriage there will be many new adjustments. Occupational choices will determine where you live. The amount of income will determine how you live. Finishing an educational degree may be necessary, which will put things on hold for a while. Limited financial resources are usually a wake-up call for young married couples. Two can not live as cheap as one, unless one does not plan to eat. The birth of a child either planned or unexpected will definitely bring the world as you knew it to a screeching halt. Living away from your parents for the first time may be a major adjustment. All these new experiences will require a constant reassessment of your priorities.

If your marriage is to start and finish on a strong foundation, always keep your relationship to God followed by your relationship to your spouse as the two top priorities in your life. Your spiritual growth together will provide stability and strength when you find it necessary to make those adjustments. If you attended church before marriage, be sure to continue after marriage. The temptation to sleep in on Sunday morning will rob each of you of the much-needed spiritual nourishment that is vital to the overall health of a marriage. In addition, attending church will put you in contact with other couples your age. This is a great source for developing relationships with others who share your faith and have similar interests.

Read

Psalm 37:4, "Delight yourself also in the LORD, and He shall give you the desires of your heart."

Matthew 6:33, "But seek first the kingdom of God and His righteousness, and all these things shall be added to you."

Reflect

_____

_____

_____

_____

Relate

What were the priorities of your marriage on your wedding day? What are they now? What are you each doing to maintain those priorities? It is important that you have a regular checkup to make sure that each is on the same page and in the same book.

37

Be Sensitive Not Stubborn

Stubbornness is only a sign of strength when it comes to standing firm for that which is right and good. The smallest amount of common sense is needed to make that choice. Otherwise, obstinacy becomes a source of pride, which leads people to think they can do no wrong.

Pride and stubbornness are double first cousins. A stubborn person is like a bass drum in that both sound loud only because of the emptiness inside. A husband or wife who is obstinate resembles a pit bull that only lets go after the damage is done both to the dog and the victim.

Being sensitive enough to admit we are wrong leads to the healing of a relationship. Many a marriage has dissolved and passed down the drain of stubbornness and pride. A stubborn husband or wife who insists they are always right thinks of no one but themselves.

The opposite of pride is humility. Pride gives a high opinion of self. Humility gives a high opinion of others. Pride springs from self-imposed ignorance. Humility is born from wisdom. Pride hardens the heart and hurts the marriage. Humility softens the heart and heals the hurts. Pride is deaf to the feelings and needs of others. Humility listens and seeks to help. Pride rejects the voice of truth, the counsel of reason, and the commands of Holy Scripture. Humility receives truth, counsel, and God's Word when spoken with pure motives and wrapped in love. After all, Jesus chose a clinging vine not a sturdy olive tree to teach us about our relation to Him. He chose a defenseless lamb not a dominate lion when His earthly ministry was introduced on the banks of the river Jordan. God chose a scrub bush not a lofty cedar to reveal himself to Moses.

A husband or wife who allows stubbornness and pride to control their lives is truly not in control of their marriage. These two vices changed angels into demons. Humility gives people the attribute of the angels. Someone once said that a humble person is like a good fruit tree—the fuller of fruit the branches are, the lower they bend themselves.

A marriage built on service and humility rather than stubbornness and pride resembles a towering redwood. When the winds howl and the rains descend, the mighty tree stands throughout the seasons because it is anchored by its roots which are well beneath the surface. Build your marriage on the virtues of life and not the vices.

Read

Job 6:24, "Teach me, and I will hold my tongue; cause me to understand wherein I have erred."

James 5:19-20, "Brethren, if anyone among you wanders from the truth, and someone turns him back, let him know that he who turns a sinner from the error of his way will save a soul from death and cover a multitude of sins."

Reflect

_____

_____

_____

_____

Relate

Are there areas in your life where stubbornness dominates? Has pride created cracks in the foundation of your marriage? Remember, what rests below the surface determines the strength of what stands above.

38

Be Responsible with Your Finances

A young couple who had been married only two years divorced due to the inability of the husband to control his spending habits. He was an attorney, and she was a fashion designer. Their combined salary was in the upper 10 percent, yet the very thing they had the most of left them empty and alone. When is enough, enough?

According to Crown Financial Ministries, Americans purchased more than two trillion dollars worth of goods and services on credit in 2004. Just imagine what that amount is today. Three-fifths of American families can not pay off their credit card debts each month, and each family has a balance of approximately $12,000. There are more than 131,000,000 sites on the Internet that deal with personal debt. The average American family is more than $84,000 in debt.

We buy without the resources to pay. Our outgo exceeds our income, which will eventually be our downfall. The strain that unpaid bills put on a marriage is tremendous. The phone calls from collecting agencies at dinnertime soon become a nightmare. Frustration leads to anger. The blame game is played. Communication breaks down. Wives yell. Husbands scream. Children cry. The marriage dissolves. Debt has taken its toll.

If at all possible, live each month on last month's wages. This will keep your mailbox empty of past due bills. The day is fast approaching when our nation may enter a time of financial stress unlike anything our grandparents every witnessed. Individuals, families, companies, and a nation can not continue to spend as if there is no tomorrow. There will definitely be a payday someday.

One simple biblical principle that most Christians fail to practice is tithing. The Old Testament standard was 10 percent of the crops and herds. The New Testament does not have a set standard. It simply says that the Lord loves a cheerful giver (2 Cor. 9:7), which means someone who gives with enthusiasm or laughter. I can not remember ever seeing anyone getting excited when the offering plate was passed in church, except the little children. If you will return to God's work a portion of the blessings with which He has blessed you, you will be amazed at how much further the remainder of your finances will go. God simply deserves to be paid first, and he promises to reward those who do so (Matt. 6:31-34).

How much money do people need? When they have plenty of food, plenty of clothes, and a comfortable house in which to live, what else is there? Why do some people always crave more? The answer is very simple. The glitz, glamour, and gold trappings of the world have replaced the goodness, grace, and giving of the heart. When a husband or wife has their eyes set on worldly possessions, they can not see what is most valuable. Marriage partners who get blinded by the sparkle of the gems, the intoxication of the wines, the seductions of the senses, and the lure of the luxuries are as lasting as names written in water.

Read

Proverbs 3:9-10, "Honor the LORD with your possessions and with the first fruits of all your increase. So your barns will be filled with plenty, and your vats will overflow with new wine."

Romans 13:8, "Owe no one anything except to love one another, for he who loves another has fulfilled the law."

Reflect

_____

_____

_____

_____

Relate

Do you and your spouse live on a budget? Are you each responsible with your monthly income? Are either or both of you in excessive debt? If so, I suggest you contact a certified Christian financial counselor through your church or contact the American Association of Christian Counselors at 1-800-526-8673.

39

Discover the Source
of True Wealth

As the old adage goes, "Whatever a man makes he leaves behind." The richest man or woman in the world may be buried in a gold casket and entombed in a marble mausoleum, but they will not take a single penny with them into eternity. Those who live in luxury and those who live in poverty enter and leave this world the same. Death comes equal to us all and makes us all equal when it comes.

The source of true wealth is not measured in art, bonds, gems, land, oil, securities, or stocks. It is not found on Wall Street or Rodeo Drive. It is not found by wearing Armani, Gucci, Dior, Lauren, or Valentino. It is not found by driving a Ferrari, Lamborghini, Bentley, Porsche, Aston Martin, or Rolls-Royce. It is not found in a partnership with a firm, but rather in a relationship with a Man. His name is Jesus. His teachings on riches and wealth are simple yet most profound. His standards for success are paradoxical to the criteria of the world.

Selfishness and greed are the archenemies of financial freedom. This one area creates more conflict in a marriage than anything else. Many married couples believe that more is better. In fact, if they could see how little wealth can buy, they would understand the value of contentment (1 Tim. 6:6). People become rich not by what they have, but by what they are. Riches and righteousness are very seldom found in the same individual or marriage.

Money will buy plenty, but not peace; money will furnish your house, but not fill your life; money will provide the best health care, but not restore your health; money will surround you with many acquaintances, but not one true friend; money will silence your accusers, but not your conscience; money will open doors, but not guarantee respect; money will remove debt, but not stress; money can purchase the service of others, but not salvation from God.

In Mark 8:36–37 Jesus asked a very penetrating question concerning riches: "For what will it profit a man if he gains the whole world, and loses his own soul? Or what will a man give in exchange for his soul?" The same could be said about a marriage. What good would it be if you gained wealth beyond belief and lost your marriage? A faithful, devoted, loving husband and wife are priceless (Prov. 31:10).

Living for wealth comes with warnings. There is a burden in getting rich; a fear in staying rich; a temptation in misusing riches; guilt in abusing riches; a sorrow in losing riches; and a fear in knowing you will be accountable for the way you used riches. Everything comes with a price tag. And there is a high price to be paid for low living.

Do not be envious of other couples who appear to have more of the world's toys. What you don't know is that many of these couples are living from paycheck to paycheck just to afford the interest payments on their toys. One month without any income, and they are in bankruptcy.

Read

Proverbs 11:24, "There is one who scatters, yet increases more; and there is one who withholds more than is right, but it leads to poverty."

Matthew 6:19, 21, "Do not lay up for yourselves treasures on earth, where moth and rust destroy and where thieves break in and steal. . . . For where your treasure is, there your heart will be also."

Reflect

_____

_____

_____

_____

Relate

In light of the above scriptures, discuss with your spouse what you treasure most and how you are using those treasures. Have you each discovered the source of true wealth? If so, are you seeking God's guidance in how you invest your riches?

40

Develop a Sense
of Healthful Humor

Healthful humor stimulates wit and stirs up laughter. It creates closeness and intimacy between people. Hurtful humor creates pain and distance. Healthful humor and laughter are never used to cause pain, but spring from the smiles which originate in the heart and explode in the face. Humor brings a spice to marriage that has it own unique scent.

A doctor friend once told me that people who have a genuine sense of humor seldom have ulcers. Laughter releases stress and puts circumstances in perspective. When we laugh, natural killer cells that destroy tumors and viruses increase, along with gamma interferon (a disease-fighting protein), T cells (helpful to the immune system), and B cells (which make disease-fighting antibodies). Laughter also lowers blood pressure, increases oxygen in the blood, and promotes healing in the body. Laughter gives the body a good interior workout.

Laughter can be great exercise for the diaphragm, as well as abdominal, respiratory, facial, leg, and back muscles. It massages abdominal organs, tones intestinal functioning, and strengthens the muscles that hold the abdominal organs in place. Not only does laughter give the midsection a workout, it can benefit digestion and absorption functioning as well. It is estimated that hearty laughter can burn calories equivalent to several minutes on the rowing machine or the exercise bike. So, instead of purchasing an expensive piece of exercise equipment, just buy some good, clean, funny videos and laugh yourself fit in body and mind. Laughing is better than sweating.

We have two choices when the everyday challenges of marriage and raising children start to weigh us down; we can search for the humor and get better, or dwell on the circumstances and become bitter. Abraham Lincoln said in those dark days of his presidency during the Civil War, "With the fearful strain that is on me night and day, if I did not laugh I should die."

When tragedy strikes a marriage, as in severe illness or death, the memories of the happy, humorous times filled with laughter and joy will serve as a source of strength. The laughter of children will echo throughout the years when the rooms stand empty and the trophies sit gathering dust. When your spouse of many years has departed this world, those occasions of humor will be engraved on your heart and will live again as fresh as the moment you laughed together.

The scriptures tell us in Proverbs 17:22, "A merry heart does good, like medicine." Laughter is truly the best medicine. It is one of God's gifts.

Read

Psalm 126:2, "Then our mouth was filled with laughter, and our tongue with singing."

Ephesians 5:19-20, "Speaking to one another in psalms and hymns and spiritual songs, singing and making melody in your heart to the Lord, giving thanks always for all things to God the Father in the name of our Lord Jesus Christ."

Reflect

_____

_____

_____

_____

Relate

Tonight at the dinner table ask someone to share a funny memory of some special event. You may be surprised what they remember. Ask your spouse to do the same before going to bed.

41

Abstain from Harmful Habits

Anything that has the potential of destroying a marriage must be avoided at all costs. Abstinence may not be a politically correct word, but it is essential when it comes to strengthening a marriage.

The number one drug problem in the United States is alcohol. According to the U.S. Department of Health and Human Services: approximately 14 million Americans—7.4 percent of the population—meet the diagnostic criteria for alcohol abuse or alcoholism; more than one-half of American adults have a close family member who has or has had alcoholism; approximately one in four children younger than eighteen years old in the United States is exposed to alcohol abuse or alcohol dependence in the family. The majority of children and teenagers take their first drink of alcohol not with their peers but in their own homes. It has been recently reported that there are more teenage alcoholics in the United States than adult alcoholics. It has been proven time and again that if one or both of the parents drink, the chances are far greater the children will follow suit.

According to the Core Institute, an organization that surveys college drinking practices, 300,000 of today's college students will eventually die of alcohol-related causes such as drunken driving accidents, cirrhosis of the liver, various cancers, and heart disease.

It is estimated that 159,000 of today's first-year college students will drop out of school next year for alcohol- or other drug-related reasons. The average student spends about $900 on alcohol each year and about $450 on books. The National Institute of Health reports that 40 percent of those who start drinking before the age of fifteen will meet the criteria for alcohol dependence at some point in their lives.

If for no other reason than the future of our children, husbands and wives and fathers and mothers should avoid the use of alcohol.

Another extremely harmful habit is Internet pornography. This is the number one addiction among men in America. It is doing more to destroy the marriages in our nation than any other self-destructive addiction. There are more pornographic Web sites on the Internet than any other. Some 20 percent of the men in our nation and 13 percent of the women look at pornography while at work. Studies reveal that 72 percent of the men and 28 percent of the women in the United States visit pornographic Web sites each month. So, it is not just a male-husband addiction. Revenue from pornography is more than the combined revenues of all professional football, baseball, and basketball franchises, and its income exceeds the combined revenues of ABC, CBS, and NBC.

If you are involved in this erotopathic lifestyle, my suggestion to you is simple—stop it! It will destroy your marriage. It will destroy your relationship with your children. It will destroy you.

If you wish to strengthen your marriage, begin with avoiding those things that will weaken it. I have briefly addressed only two harmful habits. You can make your own list.

Read

Proverbs 5:21, "For the ways of a man are before the eyes of the LORD, and He ponders all his paths."

Romans 13:12, "The night is far spent, the day is at hand. Therefore let us cast off the works of darkness, and let us put on the armor of light."

Reflect

_____

_____

_____

_____

Relate

Are there any habits in your personal life that are causing conflict in your marriage? If so, are you willing to take the necessary steps to break those habits? If not, rather than strengthening your marriage you are destroying its foundation, and eventually it will collapse. There is help and hope if you will seek it.

42

Be There for Each Other

If you belong to any organizations that require you to be away from your spouse and family during the week, resign from most of them. I know husbands and wives who are at church three nights a week plus Sunday. That is too much church activity even for the pastor.

You do not impress God by neglecting your family. You only impress Him when you are obedient to His Word. Success begins at home and not with some civic, fraternal, or religious organization. Too many husbands and wives steal time from those who love them the most to give it to those who love them the least. A lost opportunity can never be relived regardless of how many pictures the other spouse may have taken. Sitting alone at home night after night while the other spouse is involved in some outside activity gets old real fast. If you are out every night, do not be surprised if someone else takes your spouse out. Neglecting your spouse speaks volumes, and they all say the same thing, "You are not important to me anymore." Few things are sadder than a married person who is unloved and neglected. Eventually the cords will snap, and the vows will break.

Let me suggest that you and your spouse either go out to dinner, or take a weekend off together, and just talk about the things you both personally enjoy without any disapproving comments. Then make a list of those activities and find what you have in common and begin to do those things together. This will require some give and take, but that is what you did during the dating days. It is even more important to practice this kind of open exchange and shared activity during the years of marriage.

Leaving Post-it notes is not the same as talking face-to-face. Passing each other going out the door is not the same as having that much-needed date. Sending text messages is not the same as hearing each other's voice.

It takes effort and determination not to allow the small things to get in the way. You guarded your time jealously when you were dating, so keep it up. Being married to a stranger is no fun. It takes commitment to keep each other your main priority regardless of the consequence. You made a choice to come together. You must make a choice to stay together. Except for unforeseen circumstances it is vital that you be there for each other at all times. No one can take the place of the one with whom you exchanged vows.

Read

Amos 3:3, "Can two walk together, unless they are agreed?"

Ephesians 5:15-16, "See then that you walk together circumspectly [carefully], not as fools but as wise, redeeming the time, because the days are evil."

Reflect

_____

_____

_____

_____

Relate

Share with each other a special time in your marriage when you were there for each other and what it meant to you. Are there any adjustments that need to be made in order for you to spend more time together? If so, are you willing to make the necessary adjustments? What is the next event in your life when you will need the presence of your spouse? Have you shared this fact with them?

43

Learn the Difference between Fact and Feeling

Your spouse should be your best friend. Best friends spend time together. And if you spend time together, you must be able to communicate. Since communication is mostly the tone of the voice and nonverbal expressions, it would be wise if you could distinguish fact from feeling.

Husbands usually deal with facts and only secondarily with feelings, if at all. Wives deal with facts and feelings with a heavy emphasis on feelings. When a husband asks his wife how she feels about a certain thing, unless he is a very sensitive guy he doesn't hear below the surface. She makes a statement, and he takes it at face value without ever looking at her face or listening to the tone of her voice.

A television commercial captured this concept extremely well. The wife walked into the kitchen where the husband was eating his cereal and reading the paper. She held up a dress and asked, "Does this dress make me look fat?" Without looking at her or listening to the hidden message behind the question, he simply said, "You betcha." He never saw it coming. She wanted his opinion (fact) plus the assurance that she was not overweight (feeling) with emphasis on the latter. What she received was a slam to her self-image and disregard for her feelings. What he got was a long day and an even longer night in the doghouse.

Feelings are based on emotions, which are ever changing. Many couples exchange their wedding vows based strictly on their feelings for each other. They bring their hearts to the altar and leave their heads in the parking lot. Feelings will not sustain a marriage when facts overrule the emotions.

If you don't believe it, try defining "love." The majority of the words you will use are feelings.

A young man pointed out a certain young lady in a crowd and told me with great enthusiasm, "I love her!" When I asked him how he knew, he replied, "Every time I get around her I get this strange feeling in the pit of my stomach, and I can't talk, and my hands get sweaty, and I feel funny all over." I jokingly told him he might be allergic to her.

When I ask engaged couples why they want to get married, it is always the same answer, "We love each other." When I ask them how they can be sure, they respond with feeling words. Of course, love is a feeling. This is why poets and songwriters have never been able to exhaust its description. However, in addition to the multitude of feelings involved in falling in love, the fact is that without commitment most couples will not stay in love. Love without commitment is only feelings masquerading as fact.

Read

Proverbs 4:1, "Hear, my children, the instruction of a father, and give attention to know understanding."

Mark 4:9, "And He said to them, 'He who has ears to hear, let him hear!'"

Reflect

_____

_____

_____

_____

Relate

Before you go to bed tonight give your spouse a piece of paper with the numbers one through twenty written on it. Then take a similar page for yourself. Start at the same time and see which one of you can list ten positive and negative feelings first. I will get you started with one of each: positive feelings—affection; negative feelings—loneliness. Share your answers and discuss the difference between feeling and facts. There are at least 160 different feelings an individual can experience. That's a fact.

44

Speak the Words
of Love Every Day

The three most powerful words in any language are "I love you." What the individual who is speaking these words means is the key to understanding the words of love.

One person may say, "I love you," and simply mean, "I want to have sexual relations with you." That is the lowest form of the meaning of love, expressed by the Greek word *eros*. It is where we get the word "erotic." It is used to get personal pleasure and often involves little or no care about the person to whom it is spoken.

Another person may say, "I love you," referring to brotherly love; thus expressing the Greek word, *phileo*, as in Philadelphia, the city of brotherly love.

Then one may say, "I love you," and mean "I am devoted to you; I love you more than my own life." This is the Greek word *agape,* and it is the strongest of the three words for love. All three words certainly apply to the language of marriage. However, if "agape" love is missing, the marriage will be neither hot nor cold. It will have the frame without the foundation.

C. S. Lewis in *Mere Christianity* said: "They [the Christian couple] can retain this love even when each would easily, if they allowed themselves, be 'in love' with someone else. 'Being in love' first moved them to promise fidelity: this quieter love enables them to keep the promise. It is on this love that the engine of marriage is run: being in love was the explosion that started it."

In other words, falling in love through emotion is the turning of the ignition, while staying in love out of faithfulness and commitment is the fuel that moves the vehicle. It is one thing to begin a marriage. It is another to keep it going strong to the finish.

When we lived in Florida one of the orange juice companies had a slogan that said, "A day without orange juice is like a day without sunshine." In a marriage, a day without saying "I love you" to your spouse is also like a day without sunshine. We should say it with an exclamation point, not a question mark! Love is a choice.

There is no such thing as a perfect marriage because there are no perfect husbands and wives. However, in a Christian marriage the spiritual health of the marriage is directly proportional to the husband's and wife's love for God. Jesus, God's only Son, chose to love (agape) humanity to the extent that he died for our sins. Not only did he go to the cross, he rose from the grave. Can you have a great marriage without knowing Jesus? Absolutely. Can you know the depth of true love and have the best marriage possible without knowing Jesus? Absolutely not.

Read

Proverbs 5:19, "Always be enraptured with [your spouse's] love."

Philippians 1:6, "Being confident of this very thing, that He who has begun a good work in you will complete it until the day of Jesus Christ."

Reflect

_____

_____

_____

_____

Relate

Discuss with your spouse the meaning of the three words mentioned above which describe love. Which of the three is the most important and why? In what ways has agape love been shown in your marriage? Make a vow to share every day those three powerful words, "I love you!"

A Personal Word from Jerry Drace

It is my prayer for you that your life and marriage will be centered on the love of Jesus. If you have never personally invited Jesus Christ to forgive you of your sins and become your Lord and Savior, would you do that right now? The Bible says, "Today, if you will hear His voice, do not harden your hearts" (Heb.3:15; 4:7). The most important question you will ever answer is not, "Who did you marry?" but, "What did you do with Jesus?"

Romans 3:23, says, "For all have sinned and fallen short of the glory of God."

Romans 6:23, says, "For the wages of sin is death, but the gift of God is eternal life in Jesus Christ our Lord."

Romans 5:8, says, "But God demonstrates His own love toward us, in that while we were yet sinners, Christ died for us."

Romans 10:9-10, says, "If you confess with your mouth the Lord Jesus and believe in your heart that God has raised Him from the dead, you will be saved. For with the heart one believes to righteousness, and with the mouth confession is made to salvation."

Romans 10:13 says, "Whoever calls upon the name of the LORD shall be saved."

Right now, you can call upon Jesus for the forgiveness of your sins. If you are willing to do so, simply ask Him to come into your heart and forgive you of your sins. Thank Him for the gift of salvation and for the Holy Spirit.

If you have asked Jesus into your life, this is just the beginning of a journey that will last for eternity. Be sure to attend a Bible-believing, Bible-preaching church this Sunday and share your decision with the pastor. You must now get involved in the Word of God and allow the scriptures to build your life and strengthen your marriage.

God bless you,
Jerry